Daniel's
70 Weeks

By Dr. Chuck Missler

Koinonia House

Daniel's 70 Weeks
© Copyright 2015 Koinonia House Inc.
Published by Koinonia House
P.O. Box D
Coeur d'Alene, ID 83816-0347
www.khouse.org

ISBN: 978-1-57821-574-4

All Scripture quotations are from the King James Version of the Holy Bible.

PRINTED IN THE UNITED STATES OF AMERICA

Table of Contents

DANIEL'S 70 WEEKS

By Dr. Chuck Missler

Introduction

Daniel 9 is probably one of the most pivotal chapters in the entire Bible for understanding end-time prophecy. That may seem like an exaggeration, but after seeing what's packed into this chapter it will be easier to understand why that perspective is held by so many.

Daniel 9 is only one of twelve chapters, so we should start with some context. The first six chapters are historical. In those chapters we read that Daniel is deported from Israel after the Babylonian conquest. He encounters King Nebuchadnezzar, correctly interprets his dream, and is promoted as a result. Then we see Daniel's rivals trying to "undo" his three friends in the fiery furnace episode.

Nebuchadnezzar, the king of the world at that time, writes chapter four of Daniel in which he recounts his lesson from God about pride. That makes Nebuchadnezzar the only Gentile writer in the Old Testament. Next, the fall of Babylon to Darius leads us into the Persian Empire period.

After the first six chapters, we have six chapters that are a collection of Daniel's visions. They are, in a sense, appended at the end of the history. They're not in chronological order; the chapters appear as a group.

In the first chapter of that group, chapter seven, we have the *times of the Gentiles*. In chapter eight, the ram and the goat are described in a vision about the career of Alexander the Great as he defeats the Persians. That leads us into chapter nine and the seventy weeks.

It's interesting, chapters two through the end of seven are not written in Hebrew; they're in Aramaic. The author uses Aramaic because those chapters focus on the Gentile world. It's very unusual for the Bible to do that because Scripture usually sees everything, past and future, through the lens of Israel. This is a section that very unabashedly focuses on the Gentile world, and that's one reason it is so dear to us.

This is a very exciting book, but again, it's not in chronological order. The visions in Daniel seven and eight occur between the events in chapters four and five, and the interview with an archangel in chapter nine occurs between the events of chapters five and six.

Chapter 1
Background and Context

Before we get to chapter nine, it's important for us to get another perspective—a perspective coming directly from Jesus. Then we will look at the events leading up to Gabriel's words about the seventy weeks. All of this will help demonstrate what God did in order to deliver this amazing prophecy.

Matthew 24: Jesus' Perspective

In Matthew 24-25, Mark 13, and Luke 21, Jesus gave a confidential briefing on His second coming to four special disciples. According to Mark, they were Peter, James, John, and Peter's brother Andrew. This talk was important enough that it was recorded in three gospels, and it had a direct connection with Daniel's prophecy.

Matthew's account offers more information than the others, most likely due to a skill he had and the others didn't. He was a customs official, and it was a job requirement that he take shorthand. Most people are unaware that shorthand was a skill prevalent in those days.

Matthew wrote:

> *And as he [Jesus] sat upon the mount of Olives,*
> *the disciples came unto him privately, saying, Tell us,*
> *when shall these things be? and what shall be the sign*
> *of thy coming, and of the end of the world?*

Matthew 24:3

So they ask Jesus three questions, and He then gives them a two-chapter answer. The next verse gives a flavor of His answer.

Verse four reads:

> *Jesus answered and said unto them "Take heed that*
> *no man deceive you."*

Matthew 24:4

Underline that word *deceive* because He opens and closes this briefing to His disciples by warning them not to be deceived.

How do we protect ourselves from being deceived? There are all kinds of people spreading all kinds of viewpoints. But which are correct? We discern the truth by diligence, and by comparing Scripture with Scripture. Our ultimate refuge is always the whole counsel of God. Any particular perspective must be consistent with what we find in the Bible.

> *And Jesus answered and said unto them, Take heed*
> *that no man deceive you. For many shall come in*
> *my name, saying, I am Christ; and shall deceive*
> *many. And ye shall hear of wars and rumours*

of wars: see that ye be not troubled: for all these
things must come to pass, but the end is not yet.
For nation shall rise against nation, and kingdom
against kingdom: and there shall be famines,
and pestilences, and earthquakes, in divers places.
All these are the beginning of sorrows.

Matthew 24:4-8

Many, many people view these issues as signs heralding His coming, except He says these are not signs. These are *non-signs*. These things will all happen, "but the end is not yet."

The word *sorrows* there is actually *birth pains*. Mothers know what that's about. These events start slowly and increase in frequency and intensity. "But the end is not yet," according to Jesus. Then He gives the key event in the whole scenario.

The Key Event

One caveat should be made here. Remember, Jesus is clearly talking to His Jewish disciples. He is not talking to those of us who are believers under the New Covenant. That's an important distinction as we move forward.

When ye therefore shall see the abomination
of desolation, spoken of by Daniel the prophet,
stand in the holy place, (whoso readeth, let him
understand:) Then let them which be in Judaea
flee into the mountains:

Matthew 24:15

As readers, we don't want to miss our instruction here; "Whoso readeth, let him understand." This passage will be a little technical, but it's not intended for just pastors or specialists— it's intended for everyone. As we move through this topic, know that God intends for each person to understand it.

This is a good place to put to rest a controversy that began in the nineteenth century. Some critics, even today, have maintained that the book of Daniel was written by several people. Well, according to this passage, we know who wrote the book of Daniel; it was Daniel. We know this is true because that's what Jesus said was true.

With His clear statement, Jesus has saved every student of Scripture hours of tedious library research. And, that leads me to a familiar comment. If you believe in Jesus Christ, you know who wrote the book of Daniel. If you don't believe in Jesus Christ, you've got bigger problems than the authorship of the book of Daniel!

Jesus identifies Daniel as a prophet, and He does something even more. He points to the very passage that we're studying in Daniel 9 by referring to this *abomination of desolation*. That's a technical phrase. We know a lot about it, though, because it happened specifically once before in history.

The abomination of desolation refers to an idol being placed in the Temple. An idol is always considered an abomination in the Bible, but the ultimate abomination—the abomination that makes desolate—is a pagan idol in the Holy of Holies. That happened in 167 BC, and it led to the Maccabean revolt. After three years, the Jews were able to rededicate the Temple from that outrage. Jews remember the event to this day with the celebration of Hanukkah.

There is another aspect to consider here. The abomination of desolation occurs in the Holy of Holies. Who gets to go into the Holy of Holies? Only the High Priest is allowed in, only once a year at Yom Kippur, and only after great ceremonial preparation. Jesus said, "When ye therefore shall see." How can someone in Judea see this happen, and consequently know when to "flee into the mountains"? They would have to see it on cable news, of course.

In other words, this is a major political event that happens inside the Holy of Holies, inside the Temple. That's how we know there will be a temple standing; it has to be standing for this to happen. If it's televised, there will be a worldwide audience.

It is the people in Judea who are to flee, not those in New York or Moscow, but those who are in Judea. Why?

We need to understand what's going on here; the abomination of desolation is a major trigger-point in this prophecy. To make sense of this we have to go to the passage that Jesus is pointing them to in Daniel and understand the context.

The Flight from Judea

Jesus said:

> *Then let them which be in Judaea flee into the*
> *mountains: Let him which is on the housetop not*
> *come down to take any thing out of his house.*

Matthew 24:16-17

Houses in Israel are typically on hillsides because it's very hilly terrain. The roof is the patio, sort of a fellowship place. That's where they spend the cool of the evening, not in the backyard. They have to go downstairs to get to the bedrooms and all the rest of the house.

When Jesus tells them to "not come down," He's saying "Split—and do it now!"

> *Neither let him which is in the field return back to*
> *take his clothes. And woe unto them that are with*
> *child, and to them that give suck in those days!*
> *But pray ye that your flight be not in the winter,*
> *neither on the sabbath day.*

Matthew 24:18-20

Jesus also warns them about trying to grab supplies; even things like essential clothing would delay them and be a burden. It would be a handicap they couldn't afford as they flee for their lives.

Notice that His last comment refers to Sabbath; He is not talking to Gentiles. Keep in mind that the focus is on Israel and the Jews, not Gentiles. He is directing this to His disciples, who are Jewish, but it's obviously yet future. Most people don't fully recognize the "Jewishness" of Matthew 24.

The Great Tribulation

Jesus goes on to say:

> *For then shall be great tribulation, such as was not since the beginning of the world to this time, no, nor ever shall be.*

Matthew 24:21

He is quoting from Daniel 12. We'll look at that shortly, but Jesus Himself labels the last half of that seven year period as the great tribulation.

Then He makes another statement:

> *And except those days should be shortened, there should no flesh be saved: but for the elect's sake those days shall be shortened.*

Matthew 24:22

That's a technology statement; it's an allusion to advanced weapons. If someone read verse twenty-two during the 1800s, it wouldn't mean much. They couldn't imagine the world wiping itself out with muskets and bayonets, but today the nuclear cloud hangs over every geopolitical decision made on Earth. It is now possible to envision that "no flesh be saved."

Chapter 9: Daniel, Jeremiah, Gabriel

With that context established, we are ready for Daniel 9. In this chapter of Daniel, we have what is known as *the interrupted prayer.*[1] Daniel is praying in the first nineteen verses of this chapter, but then the angel Gabriel appears and interrupts his prayer. Gabriel proceeds to give Daniel the most astonishing four verses in the entire Bible: 24, 25, 26, and 27.

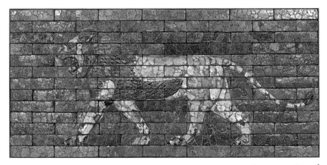

Passing Lion[2]

The Interrupted Prayer

Most people jump right into those four verses, but this is too important to cut corners. So we will start with Daniel's prayer in verse one.

> *In the first year of Darius the son of Ahasuerus, of the seed of the Medes, which was made king over the realm of the Chaldeans; In the first year of his reign I Daniel understood by books the number of the years, whereof the word of the LORD came to Jeremiah the prophet, that he would accomplish seventy years in the desolations of Jerusalem.*
>
> Daniel 9:1-2

The first verse covers titles and royal successions. Some people believe that Darius was the uncle of Cyrus, but that's conjecture by the scholars.

Other speculations are connected to the comment that he was *made* king, which implies he is a passive recipient of some kind. Setting aside these minor points, we want to look at the important part of this, which is in verse two.

This all starts because Daniel was reading his Bible, the book of Jeremiah. Please take note that Daniel took Jeremiah literally. When Jeremiah talks about seventy years in captivity, it wasn't allegorical. It wasn't about an approximate number of years, either. Daniel assumes it's precise, and he knows that the seventy years are about over.

If a believer today were reading in the Bible and somehow discovered that the Lord was coming back to the Earth three weeks from now, what would he or she do? Would they put their feet up on a desk; would they say, "Good, the sooner the better"?

That's not what Daniel would do; he would pray. He's an example to us all. He knew seventy years was prophesied in Jeremiah 25:11, and he knew about sixty-seven years had gone by. So he knew the seventy years were about over, and he's getting excited. As we go through this chapter, notice carefully what he did.

The book of Jeremiah makes reference to seventy years in two places:

And this whole land shall be a desolation, and an astonishment; and these nations shall serve the king of Babylon seventy years. And it shall come to pass,

*when seventy years are accomplished, that I will
punish the king of Babylon, and that nation, saith
the LORD, for their iniquity, and the land of the
Chaldeans, and will make it perpetual desolations.*

Jeremiah 25:11-12

*For thus saith the LORD, That after seventy years
be accomplished at Babylon I will visit you, and
perform my good word toward you, in causing you
to return to this place.*

Jeremiah 29:10

This was written in Jerusalem. So twice in the book
of Jeremiah we have this promise that Daniel could
cling to, that the captivity was about over. What does
Daniel do? Let's take a lesson here. He says:

*And I set my face unto the Lord God, to seek
by prayer and supplications, with fasting,
and sackcloth, and ashes.*

Daniel 9:3

Are we supposed to pray for the second coming
of Christ? We know the Second Coming is going
to happen; it's inevitable. But the Lord taught us
to pray, "Thy kingdom come" (Matthew 6:10).
Prayer is God's way of enlisting us in what He's doing.
Carefully consider what that should mean in your life.

Daniel also sought God by fasting. Is it appropriate
for New Testament Christians to fast? Some might say
that fasting was only for the Old Testament times,
but we repeatedly find allusions to New Testament
Christians fasting:

Then came to him the disciples of John, saying,
Why do we and the Pharisees fast oft, but thy
disciples fast not? And Jesus said unto them,
Can the children of the bridechamber mourn,
as long as the bridegroom is with them? but the
days will come, when the bridegroom shall be
taken from them, and then shall they fast.

Matthew 9:14-15

As they ministered to the Lord, and fasted,
the Holy Ghost said, Separate me Barnabas and
Saul for the work whereunto I have called them.
And when they had fasted and prayed, and laid
their hands on them, they sent them away.

Acts 13:2-3

The wife hath not power of her own body, but the
husband: and likewise also the husband hath not
power of his own body, but the wife. Defraud ye
not one the other, except it be with consent for a
time, that ye may give yourselves to fasting and
prayer; and come together again, that Satan tempt
you not for your incontinency.

1 Corinthians 7:4-5

But in all things approving ourselves as
the ministers of God, in much patience, in
afflictions, in necessities, in distresses, In stripes,
in imprisonments, in tumults, in labours,
in watchings, in fastings;

2 Corinthians 6:4-5

Don't casually decide to start fasting; it's best to have
some instruction first. It is an appropriate activity for

believers today—just do some homework in that area before starting.

Returning to Daniel:

> *And I prayed unto the LORD my God, and made*
> *my confession, and said, O Lord, the great and*
> *dreadful God, keeping the covenant and mercy*
> *to them that love him, and to them that keep*
> *his commandments; We have sinned, and have*
> *committed iniquity, and have done wickedly,*
> *and have rebelled, even by departing from thy*
> *precepts and from thy judgments: Neither have we*
> *hearkened unto thy servants the prophets, which*
> *spake in thy name to our kings, our princes, and*
> *our fathers, and to all the people of the land.*
>
> Daniel 9:4-6

Notice he says, "We have sinned." That's a strange thing for Daniel to say. He and Joseph are two people in the Old Testament about whom no evil is spoken (besides Christ). It doesn't mean they're sinless, but Daniel is praying earnestly not on his personal behalf alone, but for his people as well.

He continues in verse seven:

> *O Lord, righteousness belongeth unto thee, but*
> *unto us confusion of faces, as at this day; to the*
> *men of Judah, and to the inhabitants of Jerusalem,*
> *and unto all Israel, that are near, and that are*
> *far off, through all the countries whither thou*
> *hast driven them, because of their trespass that*

*they have trespassed against thee. O Lord, to us
belongeth confusion of face, to our kings, to our
princes, and to our fathers, because we have sinned
against thee. To the Lord our God belong mercies
and forgivenesses, though we have rebelled against
him; Neither have we obeyed the voice of the
LORD our God, to walk in his laws, which he set
before us by his servants the prophets. Yea, all Israel
have transgressed thy law, even by departing, that
they might not obey thy voice; therefore the curse is
poured upon us, and the oath that is written in the
law of Moses the servant of God, because we have
sinned against him.*

Daniel 9:7-11

He's saying their national destiny is determined by
their behavior. Were there some saved among them?
Of course, but that doesn't alter their national destiny,
which is a function of their national behavior.[3]

*And he hath confirmed his words, which he spake
against us, and against our judges that judged us,
by bringing upon us a great evil: for under the
whole heaven hath not been done as hath been
done upon Jerusalem. As it is written in the law of
Moses, all this evil is come upon us: yet made we
not our prayer before the LORD our God, that we
might turn from our iniquities, and understand
thy truth. Therefore hath the LORD watched upon
the evil, and brought it upon us: for the LORD our
God is righteous in all his works which he doeth:
for we obeyed not his voice. And now, O Lord our*

God, that hast brought thy people forth out of
the land of Egypt with a mighty hand, and
hast gotten thee renown, as at this day; we have
sinned, we have done wickedly. O Lord, according
to all thy righteousness, I beseech thee, let thine
anger and thy fury be turned away from thy city
Jerusalem, thy holy mountain: because for our sins,
and for the iniquities of our fathers, Jerusalem
and thy people are become a reproach to all that
are about us.

Daniel 9:12-16

All this has been an acknowledgement of sin. The focus is Jerusalem and the people of God. But notice what starts to happen as his prayer continues; it's fascinating. Even in the English, the frequency of those verbs starts picking up. We can almost feel the intensity, the emotion, the trembling of Daniel.

Now therefore, O our God, hear the prayer of thy
servant, and his supplications, and cause thy face
to shine upon thy sanctuary that is desolate, for
the Lord's sake. O my God, incline thine ear, and
hear; open thine eyes, and behold our desolations,
and the city which is called by thy name: for we
do not present our supplications before thee for our
righteousnesses, but for thy great mercies. O Lord,
hear; O Lord, forgive; O Lord, hearken and do;
defer not, for thine own sake, O my God: for thy
city and thy people are called by thy name.

Daniel 9:17-19

Gabriel's Visit

Now we get to the interruption. We're going to have a few comments by a mighty angel of God and then, of course, the incredible gift that Gabriel gives Daniel.

And whiles I was speaking, and praying,
and confessing my sin and the sin of my people
Israel, and presenting my supplication before the
LORD my God for the holy mountain of my God;
Yea, whiles I was speaking in prayer, even the man
Gabriel, whom I had seen in the vision at the
beginning, being caused to fly swiftly, touched me
about the time of the evening oblation.

Daniel 9:20-21

Notice that he shifted gears from the prayer to narrating what happened. It's interesting to see Daniel describe this. Obviously, Gabriel is one of the archangels. We only know of three that are named: Gabriel, Michael, and one named Lucifer who got into a big bunch of trouble because of his pride.

Michael is always a warrior, fighting on behalf of God's people. Gabriel is always announcing something having to do with the Messiah.

The word translated *man* here, and applied to Gabriel, is the Hebrew word, *ish*. *Ish* can mean *man* or *servant*, so this can be read as "the servant Gabriel," although he may have appeared as a man.

There is something very subtle here. Gabriel touched Daniel on the shoulder "at the time of the evening oblation." Daniel makes that reference even though the Temple is about four hundred miles to the west and in rubble. There is no temple; there is no evening oblation. It's an anachronism that's out of date by virtually seventy years, but not for Daniel.

Daniel is using a phrase here that is very revealing of his heart, and how he is thinking. As far as he's concerned, it was God's appointed time and they would be offering a sacrifice, an oblation, if they had a temple. That's when Gabriel came to him.

> *And he informed me, and talked with me, and said, O Daniel, I am now come forth to give thee skill and understanding. At the beginning of thy supplications the commandment came forth, and I am come to shew thee; for thou art greatly beloved: therefore understand the matter, and consider the vision.*

> Daniel 9:22-23

Daniel must have been thrilled. He's told that he is "greatly beloved" of God. Recall that God spoke to Moses face-to-face "as a man speaketh unto his friend" (Exodus 33:11). And what did Jesus say to the disciples in the upper room:

> *Henceforth I call you not servants; for the servant knoweth not what his lord doeth: but I have called you friends; for all things that I have heard of my Father I have made known unto you.*

> John 15:15

What does it mean to be God's friend? To His friend, God would reveal what He was going to do. He called Moses a friend and told him what was going to happen to the surrounding nations (Exodus 34). Jesus called the disciples His friends and told them about His second coming.

Is there anyone closer than a friend? Moses is known as a friend of God in the Old Testament, but who is *beloved* in the Old Testament? Daniel is beloved by God. Who is beloved in the New Testament? John is often referred to as "the disciple whom Jesus loved" in the Gospel of John. How interesting to see what comes from that kind of rapport with God. Daniel, because he's beloved, is entrusted with apocalyptic insights. In the New Testament, John is beloved, and he is granted the privilege of delivering the apocalyptic book of Revelation.

There is a consistency between the Old and the New Testament concerning relationship. A friend of God will be let in on what's coming. The beloved of God really has the inside track.

Chapter 2
Introducing Daniel 9:24-27

The material covered so far gives a context for the next four verses—the real focus of our study. We're going to now look at the seventy weeks, as found in Daniel 9:24-27. Daniel 9:24 will give the scope of the whole package: the overview. It will be followed by verse twenty-five, which is going to deal with sixty-nine of the seventy weeks. That passage will be the most startling passage in the Bible, from a prophetic point of view.

Verse twenty-seven deals with the seventieth week, which seems missing from verse twenty-five. Verse twenty-six, which obviously occurs between twenty-five and twenty-seven, deals with the events that are after the sixty-ninth week and before the seventieth week. We would naturally presume that all seventy weeks are contiguous, except for this insertion. It tells us there's something after the sixty-ninth, but before the seventieth week. There's an interval between them, and it has to last at least thirty-eight years. This interval will provide the structure of the passage.

Chapter 3
The Scope (Verse 24)

Verse twenty-four reads:

Seventy weeks are determined upon thy people and upon thy holy city, to finish the transgression, and to make an end of sins, and to make reconciliation for iniquity, and to bring in everlasting righteousness, and to seal up the vision and prophecy, and to anoint the most Holy.

Daniel 9:24

Daniel's people were the Jews, and Jerusalem is the holy city. It is in relation to them that the "seventy sevens" will result in the consummation of the six things mentioned in this verse. This is about the Jews, as we have emphasized previously.

Six Results

The first two of the six results are "to finish the transgression, to make an end of sins." Has there been "an end of sins" and has "the transgression" finished? Cable news, along with other news outlets, constantly broadcasts the answer to that question. Sin abounds in the world today.

With the next two results it might be argued that making "an end of sins," the "reconciliation for our iniquity," has been accomplished on the cross. But when combined with the next phrase, "To bring in everlasting righteousness," we have to say these results have not been fully realized.

Lastly, we have "To seal up [or complete, conclude] the vision and prophecy" and one last thing, "to anoint the most holy place." Some versions may say "the most Holy", but it is *Kaddish, Kaddishim.* This is the Holy of Holies, and apparently it's going to need some very special anointing.

The main point to draw from this is the scope of this prophecy. It is incredibly conclusive on the one hand, and yet incomplete in terms of fulfillment on the other. So the seventieth week has not been finished yet, whatever else is true.

"Weeks"

Just how long is a week? Most people are only familiar with a week of days, but there is also a *week of weeks.* That may be surprising, but you can see it in the Feast of Weeks in Leviticus 23:15-16. There is also a *week of months* from Nisan to Tishri, or from Tishri to Nisan. Either way, it's a week of months, and is ordained in Exodus 12:2 and Leviticus 23:24.

Of course, our focus is on a *week of years.* There are sabbatical years for the land, and this is emphasized in virtually all of Leviticus 25, as well as Leviticus 26 and Deuteronomy 15.

Speak unto the children of Israel, and say unto them, When ye come into the land which I give you, then shall the land keep a sabbath unto the LORD. Six years thou shalt sow thy field, and six years thou shalt prune thy vineyard, and gather in the fruit thereof; But in the seventh year shall be a sabbath of rest unto the land, a sabbath for the LORD: thou shalt neither sow thy field, nor prune thy vineyard.

Leviticus 25:2-4

In fact, when looking at 2 Chronicles 36, we discover the reason the Jews were in captivity for seventy years.

And them that had escaped from the sword carried he away to Babylon; where they were servants to him and his sons until the reign of the kingdom of Persia: To fulfil the word of the LORD by the mouth of Jeremiah, until the land had enjoyed her sabbaths: for as long as she lay desolate she kept sabbath, to fulfil threescore and ten years.

2 Chronicles 36:20-21

They didn't honor the idea of a year off for the land. That was supposed to happen every seven years, but they didn't do it for 490 years. Seventy times they ignored God's direction in the Law. Then God said, in effect, "You owe Me seventy," and He took them out of the land so it could "lay desolate" and keep the Sabbath rest. That's an example of a week of years.

We have something like that in English. If someone said he wouldn't be back for a decade, we would expect him back in ten years. We understood that expression even though the word *years* was not used. The Hebrew word *Shabuwa* (literally a seven-period) is a week, but a week of years, not days. That may sound strange, but to the Jews it was very familiar.

Chapter 4
The 69 Weeks (Verse 25)

In verse twenty-five, Gabriel says to Daniel, "Know therefore and understand." This is not a cryptic hidden thing; this is something Daniel is expected to understand.

> *Know therefore and understand, that from the going forth of the commandment to restore and to build Jerusalem unto the Messiah the Prince shall be seven weeks, and threescore and two weeks: the street shall be built again, and the wall, even in troublous times.*

Daniel 9:25

Notice the sixty-nine weeks are seven plus sixty-two. Scholars aren't quite sure why it was presented that way. One of the speculations is that it took seven weeks of years to get Jerusalem rebuilt. That's a speculation; we're not sure exactly why it is divided like that. This is a mathematical prophecy, so from one event to another is a specific period of time.

Gabriel is speaking of Jerusalem being rebuilt, but picture the context of the situation. Daniel is now an old man, in his seventies or eighties. He was deported as a teenager in the captivity. He rose to power in Babylon under Nebuchadnezzar. Then Cyrus conquered Babylon, and Daniel rose to power again in the Persian kingdom as a prime minister. He has been absent from Jerusalem his whole life, and Jerusalem is in rubble. It was destroyed decades before, but he knows from Jeremiah's prophecy that it's destined to be rebuilt. That rebuilding has been the hope of the faithful Jews all along. Now Daniel has Gabriel appearing and actually speaking to him about it. No doubt he is excited.

Then the Holy Spirit adds a footnote here; "the street shall be built again and the wall in troubled times." The Holy Spirit always anticipates every conceivable misunderstanding that might arise. We cannot encounter a false cult or a false belief on any of the landscape that isn't anticipated specifically in the Scripture. That's really amazing. Anyway, He says there will be trouble with rebuilding, and that's what is recorded in the books of Ezra and Nehemiah.

Verse twenty-five gives us both a trigger and a target. The *terminus a quo*, as a scholar would say, the beginning point (or trigger), is "from the going forth of the commandment to restore and to build Jerusalem." The *terminus ad quem*, the final conclusion (or target), is "unto the *Meshiach Nagid*, the Messiah the Prince." Between those two events is sixty-nine weeks of years (sixty-nine times seven), which is 483 years.

Decrees

Some Bibles have a footnote saying there were three different decrees, or commandments, which could qualify as the one referred to in this verse. That's wrong—there are actually four decrees:

1) Cyrus in 537 B.C. (Ezra 1:2-4)
2) Darius in 522 B.C. (Ezra 6:8)
3) Artaxerxes in 458 B.C. (Ezra 7)
4) Artaxerxes' second decree in 445 B.C. (Nehemiah 2)

There is a difference between the book of Ezra and the book of Nehemiah. The book of Ezra is the chronicle of Cyrus freeing the Jews to go home and build their temple. They struggle, and they struggle, and they struggle to build their temple, and that's what Ezra is all about. They don't get very far because they can't protect themselves. That sets the stage for Nehemiah.

Nehemiah is the cupbearer to the king, Artaxerxes. In 458 B.C., Artaxerxes issues a decree that's useful, but we're interested in the later one, the fourth one, in 445 B.C. It's recorded in three different places in Nehemiah 2. This decree stands out because it is the only one of the four decrees that deals with the city of Jerusalem. The other three are dealing only with the Temple.

"The street shall be built again, and the wall." The word for *wall* is literally a trench or moat.

The Hebrew word *rechob* means "street," and the word *charuts* means "wall or moat" in verse twenty-five. Clearly, the focus of Gabriel's trigger point is the city not the Temple. Therefore, the first three decrees are not the ones that should concern us because they deal only with the Temple, while the fourth specifically mentions the city.

Nehemiah was trusted by King Artaxerxes. He had a relationship with the king; he was the cupbearer, the taster. As a favor to Nehemiah, the king gave him the authority to rebuild the city, put a wall around it, and have a Jewish government. That was all missing from the other decrees.

Israel had been enslaved by Babylon. They were freed under Cyrus and went home. The nation was no longer under servitude, but they couldn't build their city. They didn't have the authority. Nehemiah gets that authority, and that's what Gabriel is referring to as he talks to Daniel: the decree to restore the city of Jerusalem.

It turns out that this decree, the decree of Artaxerxes Longimanus, is recorded and dated. Using our calendar, it was given on March 14, 445 B.C.

This whole presentation is indebted to Sir Robert Anderson. He published a landmark study in 1894 that tracked down a lot of these details.[4] That book was a rare book at one time, but it has become very popular. Pick it up in any good Christian bookstore: *The Coming Prince*, by Sir Robert Anderson.[5]

The trigger point, the *terminus a quo*, is the decree of Artaxerxes Longimanus on March 14, 445 B.C. With that settled, now we have to determine what kind of year is being used. There are lunar years, solar years, and sidereal years. This will be interesting.

360 Day Calendars

The Bible always deals in 360 day years. Sir Robert Anderson noted that fact, and that led to the unraveling of this verse, Daniel 9:25. In Genesis 7-8, a year consists of 12 thirty-day months. It sounds very peculiar, but the books of Daniel and Revelation deal with this too. So from Genesis to Revelation, for certain purposes at least, we're dealing in 360 day years.

As we investigate this further, it's very puzzling because all the ancient civilizations had calendars based on 360 day calendars. This includes the following:

Assyrians
Chaldeans
Egyptians
Hebrews
Persians
Greeks
Phoenicians
Chinese
Mayans
Hindus
Carthaginians
Etruscans
Teutons

They typically had 12 thirty-day months, but sometimes with slight variations. Then they all change about 701 B.C. We get into this with great detail in our commentary study of the long day of Joshua (Joshua 10:12-13). There is a conjecture, just a conjecture, by some scientists that Mars and the Earth were on resonant orbits in ancient times. The Earth had an orbit of 360 days, and Mars had one of 720 days.

Every 104 years there would be a near pass-by between Mars and Earth when the two orbits crossed. They've discovered that such an event would set up what is referred to as an *orbital resonance*. This caused something like a tuning fork effect, which transferred energy. This has all been modeled by computer, with some fascinating insights.

If the near pass-by was in the spring, on March 20 or 21, Mars would pass near the Earth from the inside (the perihelion). These were resonant orbits, so Earth would gain some energy, and Mars would lose a little energy. The orbits would alter a little bit because of this energy transfer.

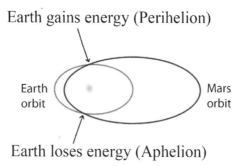

Earth gains energy (Perihelion)

Earth orbit   Mars orbit

Earth loses energy (Aphelion)

At other times, there would be a near pass-by in the fall, on October 25. Mars would come from the side farthest from the sun (the aphelion) and pass behind the Earth. The Earth would lose the energy, in that case, and Mars would pick it up.

That sounds like a simple astronomical event, but it was much more. We can't go into the details here, but every time Mars drew near there were huge, usually catastrophic, events on the Earth. That's why the ancient peoples were terrified of Mars, and some used the name for the "god of war." The name also appears in "martial" arts. People were terrified when one of these near pass-bys happened.

By 701 B.C., the Earth had picked up five and one-quarter days. Instead of a 360 day year, the Earth now had a year with 365 ¼ days. Mars lost a few days: from 720 down to 687 days. The energy transfer between Earth and Mars had finally stabilized, and this is when the calendar changes began. The Romans added 5 ¼ days to their calendar, and Hezekiah added a month to the Jewish calendar, using a cycle of seven times in a nineteen year cycle.

Near pass-bys with Mars are strangely confirmed by Jonathan Swift's fictional story *Gulliver's Travels*. Swift was an Irish poet, a satirist, and he was making fun of the politics in London with his stories.

We all know about Gulliver's voyage to Lilliput, the place of the little people. It's looked at now as just a story for children, of course, because we've lost the political context of the time.

Our interest is in the third voyage of Gulliver. He visits an island where the astronomers brag that they know about the two moons of Mars. Swift mentions their orbits and even their rotation. What makes that bizarre is that Jonathan Swift published his *Gulliver's Travels* 151 years before the astronomical world discovered there were two moons of Mars!

Telescopes had not been invented that could resolve the two moons of Mars. One moon is only eight miles across. It's almost black; it has an albedo, a reflectivity, of only three percent. They are hard to see even with a good telescope, such as we have today.[6]

Did that mean that he really knew these facts? No, he probably used some legend he had heard to embellish his stories not realizing that those legends were eyewitness accounts.

Well, there were cosmological changes apparently, but we come back to verse twenty-five and we're using 360 days here. This means Gabriel is telling Daniel that "from the commandment to restore Jerusalem, unto Messiah the King" will be 173,880 days. We reach that number using 69 *weeks* of 360 day years.

The King

When did Jesus permit Himself to be proclaimed as a king? Many times in the New Testament we read about the enthusiasm of the crowd. In John 6:15, they tried to make Him a king, but He slipped away— He wouldn't let it happen.

Then, one day, Jesus does something weird. In fact, He not only permits it, He arranges it. He intentionally sets things up to fulfill a prophecy of Zechariah.

> *Rejoice greatly, O daughter of Zion; shout,*
> *O daughter of Jerusalem: behold, thy King cometh*
> *unto thee: he is just, and having salvation; lowly,*
> *and riding upon an ass, and upon a colt the foal of*
> *an ass.*
>
> Zechariah 9:9

Jesus deliberately tells his disciples to go to a certain place to get a donkey, and He even gives them a password to use so the owner will release it. They bring it to Him, and He rides this donkey into Jerusalem to fulfill the Scripture; "Thy King cometh unto thee." He is presenting Himself as a king to Jerusalem.

We have probably all heard the verse from Psalm 118:

> *This is the day which the LORD hath made;*
> *we will rejoice and be glad in it.*
>
> Psalm 118:24

Just what does "This is the day" really mean? We can certainly rejoice for another day from the Lord, but this verse is celebrating a specific day in history.

In Luke 19, we have the triumphal entry with Jesus riding the donkey into the city. People are throwing down the palm branches, and when they run out of palm branches, they throw down their coats. They are singing a part of Psalm 118;

*Saying, Blessed be the King that cometh in the
name of the Lord: peace in heaven, and glory in
the highest.*

Luke 19:38

As Gentiles, we may listen to this and think,
"Wow, that's pretty neat." That only means we've
missed the point. And whenever we run the risk of
missing the point, the Pharisees come to our rescue.
When the Pharisees are upset, it may be for something
that we, as Gentiles, are likely to miss. They become
unglued when they hear the people praising Jesus.

*And some of the Pharisees from among
the multitude said unto him, Master, rebuke
thy disciples.*

Luke 19:39

The people were just singing a song. It's only
a psalm, why the angst? The Pharisees were very
concerned because by singing that psalm under these
circumstances, the people were declaring Jesus to be
the Messiah. The Pharisees naturally assume that this
rabbi doesn't want His disciples blaspheming by calling
Him the Messiah.

Notice His tactful reply:

*And he answered and said unto them, I tell you
that, if these should hold their peace, the stones
would immediately cry out.*

Luke 19:40

Whenever we're in Israel on a tour, we always take some pictures up at the top of the Mount of Olives; it's a great overlook of the old city. We usually walk down the road to the base of the Mount of Olives. That's the very road that Jesus used in Luke 19 because it comes from the top of the Mount of Olives.

While going down this road, everyone is encouraged to pick up a rock or two, and when they get home, they can have the rocks mounted like a trophy on a piece of walnut or something. Then when somebody asks, "What's that?" the owner can reply, "Glad you asked!" Then he or she can tell them, "That's one of the stones that didn't cry out," and then talk all about Daniel 9 and Luke 19—after all, they brought it up.

Chronologies and Calculations

So we see Jesus presented as the King, but we need the date of that event before we can say that these calculations are right. We have to consider the chronology of Christ's ministry.

We know that the Lord's ministry began in the fall of 28 A.D. How do we know that? Tiberius was appointed in 14 A.D. and Augustus died on August 19th of 14 A.D., and we know from Luke 3 that His ministry began in the fifteenth year of Tiberius, which means that we need to add fourteen plus fourteen. (The fifteenth year hadn't gone by, so only fourteen are complete.)

We can find other people who try to support a different chronology, and some may wonder why there would be any controversy. Part of the problem is they're trying to defend a Friday crucifixion—and Passover in 32 A.D. was not on a Friday. People who are trying to defend a Friday crucifixion have to use a year when Passover was on a Friday, which can be disproven by three different passages in the New Testament, but let's just stay on course.

So we have the commandment to restore and build Jerusalem with the decree of Artaxerxes Longimanus on March 14, 445 B.C. The triumphal entry occurred on April 6, 32 A.D. If we take the number of years, adding the number of days between March 14 and April 6, then go through the leap-year calculations, we will be following the steps in Sir Robert Anderson's book *The Coming Prince,* re-published in 1994. The heart of it is that the number of days between the decree that triggered the calculation and the triumphal entry that concludes it is 173,880 days.

There is one other thing. The Septuagint translation that we're drawing this from was translated into Greek less than halfway through this period. In other words, this prophecy was translated into Greek 300 years earlier. That means no one could *monkey around* with this after the fact.

What was Gabriel's margin of error? Zero; because Gabriel told Daniel the precise day that the Messiah would present Himself as a king to Jerusalem. And that's what Jesus did.

They Did Not Know The Times

We're not through with Luke 19. Jesus started in Bethany, rode the donkey up over the Mount of Olives, came down the Kidron Valley, and headed into the old city.

> *And when he was come near, he beheld the city, and wept over it, Saying, If thou hadst known, even thou, at least in this thy day, the things which belong unto thy peace! but now they are hid from thine eyes.*

> Luke 19:41-42

He wept over the city. This is the Triumphal Entry, the big day, but He wept over it. He expected them to understand that He was the Messiah because He was arriving on schedule, as Gabriel had predicted. But they didn't see that their day to usher in peace had arrived. So He essentially said, "You had your chance," and wept.

Then He says that now "the things which belong unto thy peace" are hidden from them. He announces *judicial blindness* here. Even today, Israel is blinded. Will she be blinded forever? No, Paul tells us in Romans 11:25 that Israel is blinded "until the fullness of the Gentiles come in," *i.e.* the completion of the Church.

This is a sobering passage, but it gets worse. He goes on to say:

> *For the days shall come upon thee, that thine enemies shall cast a trench about thee, and compass*

thee round, and keep thee in on every side,
And shall lay thee even with the ground, and thy
children within thee; and they shall not leave in
thee one stone upon another; because thou knewest
not the time of thy visitation.

Luke 19:43-44

Thirty-eight years after He spoke, Titus Vespasian and the 5th, 10th, 12th, and 15th Roman Legions laid siege to Jerusalem for about nine months. They slaughtered over a million inhabitants: men, women, and children. Another half-million died from the famines and pestilence which followed.

Notice the rest of verse forty-four. Jesus explains why Jerusalem fell in 70 A.D.; "because thou knewest not the time of thy visitation." That's chilling— Jesus held them accountable to know this prophecy. They may not have known the exact day, but they should have recognized the situation. They failed to give attention, and many were destroyed.

There is a responsibility that goes along with having Scripture. Today we have so much more access and understanding of Scripture and the fulfillment of prophecy. We do well to take up our responsibility for that privilege.

Chapter 5
The Interval (Verse 26)

Now here's verse twenty-six:

And after threescore and two weeks shall Messiah be cut off, but not for himself: and the people of the prince that shall come shall destroy the city and the sanctuary; and the end thereof shall be with a flood, and unto the end of the war desolations are determined.

Daniel 9:26

Remember verse twenty-five to get the context here. Gabriel previously said there were "seven weeks, and three score and two weeks." The reference here in verse twenty-six to "after three score and two weeks," confuses many people, but if we just sketch it out, it makes sense. It's like saying "after the sixty-nine weeks." It's the same thing.

"Karat"

After the sixty-nine weeks, "shall Messiah be cut off." The Hebrew word for "cut off" is *karat*, and it means "to be executed, to be killed, to be cut off." This is a prophecy that the Messiah is destined to be killed; He is to be executed for a capital crime.

Who committed a crime worthy of the death penalty? Who deserved this execution? He was executed for you and for me; we deserved the death sentence.

We have another phrase that comes up here; "the prince that shall come." Many people read this superficially and jump to the conclusion that "the prince that shall come" is the Messiah because, indeed, the Messiah has come—and shall come. But look at the context;"the people of the prince that shall come shall destroy the city and the sanctuary."

We have a 20/20 hindsight opportunity here because we know who destroyed the city and the sanctuary. What happened thirty-eight years after Christ was crucified? The Roman legions set a siege and destroyed not only the city, but the sanctuary as well. So, "the people of the prince that shall come" are obviously the Romans, and their leader, the "prince that shall come," is a Roman leader.

It's interesting that "the prince that shall come" is one of thirty-three titles of the final world ruler. Nimrod was the first such leader, and this man that's coming is the last one. There are actually thirty-three titles for him in the Old Testament and thirteen in the New Testament. Unfortunately, we seem to have chosen one of those to be sort of a catchall. We call him the Antichrist.

That name Antichrist is okay, except it's a little misleading because many people understand *anti* to mean against. He is against Christ, but the word *antichrist* in the Greek really means "instead of Christ." There are many other labels that are actually more descriptive, and one of those is "the prince that shall come." This is a ruler who will be a major player in verse twenty-seven.

In our earlier materials, we concluded that if "the prince that shall come" is from the Roman Empire, then he must be out of western Europe. There are many very competent Bible scholars that, to this day, still hold that opinion. Candidly, we may be victims of myopia.

When we think of the Roman Empire, we tend to think of Western Europe. We ignore the Eastern leg of that empire. It's so different, we give it a different name; we call it the Byzantine Empire. We use that term to refer to the eastern leg because that part of the Roman Empire outlived the western leg by a thousand years.

It was Diocletian who divided the Roman Empire into two parts because it had become so big. When Constantine took over, he was so fed up with the politics in Rome that he moved the capital of the Roman Empire, the capital of the world, to Byzantium. He named it Constantinople; it was the new Rome.

We have a tendency in cultural terms to think of the Roman Empire in its Western Europe heritage. We tend to disregard the eastern leg of the Roman Empire because of our own labeling. We know, from Isaiah 10, Micah 5, and several other passages, that one of the key titles of the antichrist is "The Assyrian." We have materials on that for those wanting to go more in-depth.[7]

Recap

Notice the diagram titled "The Interval in Daniel 9." It shows verses 25, 26 and 27. Verse 24 was the scope of the whole prophecy, so it's not listed. Verse 25, is the sixty-nine weeks, consisting of seven plus sixty-two. That's why saying "after sixty-two," is really saying "after the sixty-nine." The seventieth week is not yet; that's going to be dealt with in verse 27.

The Interval in Daniel 9

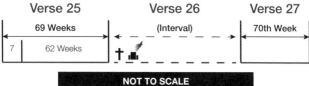

Verse twenty-six deals with an interval between the sixty-nine weeks and the seventieth week. The sixty-nine weeks include the Triumphal Entry, which was four days earlier, on the tenth of Nisan. As Jesus rode that donkey into Jerusalem, He was the Lamb of God presenting Himself for examination. Jews were examining the lambs in the Temple for Passover on that same day. Four days later, the crucifixion took place, and Messiah was "cut off." That marked the end of the sixty-nine weeks, and the beginning of this interval.

The city and the sanctuary were destroyed by "the people of the prince that shall come." We know that happened in 70 A.D., so we know, from the text alone, this interval has to include at least thirty-eight years. Since verse twenty-seven hasn't started yet, it can be argued that this interval has lasted for over 1,970 years.

Rabbinical Confirmations

We should point out that verse twenty-six was seen as *messianic* in rabbinical literature. It was to be fulfilled prior to the Temple being destroyed. Specifically, our source for this is *Yalkut, Volume 2.* In *Midrach Berishit (Warsaw Edition)*, the Messiah was to exit prior to 33 A.D. We are indebted to Yacob Prasch for his insights.

So if we're looking for a candidate for the Messiah of Israel, it should be somebody who was executed before the Fall of Jerusalem and prior to 33 A.D. We have a great candidate to put forward for consideration.

Israel and the Church

It will be helpful in our study to consider some distinctions between Israel and the Church. They're different. They have different origins, different missions, and they certainly have very different destinies. Failure to see these differences can lead to some very grave errors.

Destiny of Israel

These four verses in Daniel 9 are aimed at Israel, so we need to take Israel into account because it's the missing key of systematic theology.

In any pastor's library there is likely to be a set of books called *Systematic Theology,* or something equivalent. All of them have pretty much the same table of contents, even if they have different views about some things.

The table of contents would look something like this:

1) **Bibliology** (study of the Bible).
2) **Theology** (study of the attributes of God)
3) **Christology** (study of the Lord Jesus Christ)
4) **Pneumatology** (study of the Holy Spirit)
5) **Angelology** (study of angels: both fallen and holy)
6) **Anthropology** (study of man)
7) **Soteriology** (study of salvation)
8) **Ecclesiology** (study of the Church)
9) **Eschatology** (study of last things or end-time things)

It comes as a shock to discover that there is a topic which constitutes five-sixths of the Bible that is not mentioned as a study in most renderings of systematic theology. That study is **Israelology**, the study of Israel as God's instrument in His plan of redemption. It's scattered through some of the other topics, but there is no definitive focus on Israel.

Replacement Theology

It's astonishing to realize how many churches are totally obtuse to the role of Israel in the future. In fact, they embrace a concept that's called Replacement Theology.

Replacement Theology states that because Israel rejected her Messiah the promises that were made to Israel fall upon the Church now. The concept is that the Church has replaced Israel. That happens to be an unfortunate heresy for several reasons. It causes a lot of confusion, but more than that, it tends to make God a liar.

Verse after verse after verse reaffirms God's commitment to Israel—national Israel. This is true throughout the Old and New Testaments. Not the least of these is Gabriel's commitment to Mary that her Child would sit on David's throne. That throne didn't exist when Mary heard those words, and Jesus has yet to ascend that royal dais.

Replacement views are sometimes heard from the pulpit, and they lay the basis for anti-Semitism. It was this viewpoint that led to the Holocaust in Europe. It wasn't just the Nazis who were against the Jews; the silent pulpits were anti-Semitic in their very nature.

One rebuttal to Replacement Theology is Paul's definitive statement of Christian doctrine in the book of Romans. In it, he hammers away for three chapters (nine, ten and eleven) that God is not finished with

Israel. They have a destiny. This seventy-week prophecy deals with Israel's destiny; it does not directly involve the Church. Gabriel made that very clear right up front.

It's very helpful to notice how Paul describes the world in the New Testament period, the Church period. He separates all people into three categories: Jews, Gentiles, and the Church. Here is just one example:

> *Give none offence, neither to the Jews, nor to the Gentiles, nor to the church of God:*
>
> 1 Corinthians 10:32

Between Pentecost and the Rapture—the Church's birth and its translation to the eternal—the Church is the focus of God's program. It is neither Jew nor Gentile. Once the Church is gone, God is going to deal with people as Jew and Gentile, just as He did before the Church.

We see this in the Book of Revelation. There is a definite shift to a Jewish frame of reference beginning with Revelation 4:4. The distinction between Jews and Gentiles re-appears once the Church is in heaven. We see the change in emphasis also appearing with the use of references to the Old Testament. There are 404 verses in Revelation containing over 800 allusions from the Old Testament. The vast majority of that number comes after Revelation 4:4.

The Interval Throughout Scripture

This interval in Daniel 9:26 is also implied in other Scriptures. Perhaps the most dramatic is when Jesus, in Luke 4, reads in the synagogue at Nazareth. He opens to Isaiah 61:1-2 and reads it aloud.

> *The Spirit of the Lord is upon me, because he hath anointed me to preach the gospel to the poor; he hath sent me to heal the brokenhearted, to preach deliverance to the captives, and recovering of sight to the blind, to set at liberty them that are bruised, To preach the acceptable year of the Lord,*
>
> Luke 4:18-19

Then Jesus does a very strange thing:

> *And he closed the book, and he gave it again to the minister, and sat down. And the eyes of all them that were in the synagogue were fastened on him. And he began to say unto them, This day is this scripture fulfilled in your ears.*
>
> Luke 4:20-21

What did He leave out? Here is the passage in Isaiah; notice what comes after the comma:

> *To proclaim the acceptable year of the LORD, and the day of vengeance of our God;*
>
> Isaiah 61:2

Is that "day of vengeance" going to be fulfilled? Absolutely, it will happen. Has it been fulfilled yet? No, that comma has lasted some 2,000 years. So we can say with confidence that the interval between the sixty-ninth and seventieth weeks is implied here. We find the same interval in Revelation 12. Frankly, we can find twenty-four places in the Word of God where the interval concerning the Church is implied.[8]

The interval is defined as beginning when Jesus said:

> *If thou hadst known, even thou, at least in this thy day, the things which belong unto thy peace! but now they are hid from thine eyes.*
>
> Luke 19:42

The end of the interval is described by Paul:

> *For I would not, brethren, that ye should be ignorant of this mystery, lest ye should be wise in your own conceits; that blindness in part is happened to Israel, until the fulness of the Gentiles be come in.*
>
> Romans 11:25

The interval that we're talking about is for the Church, and that's an era that was kept secret in the Old Testament.

In Matthew, as Jesus talked about the seven kingdom parables, He said:

> *Another parable spake he unto them; The kingdom of heaven is like unto leaven, which a woman took, and hid in three measures of meal, till the whole was leavened. All these things spake Jesus unto the*

*multitude in parables; and without a parable spake
he not unto them: That it might be fulfilled which
was spoken by the prophet, saying, I will open my
mouth in parables; I will utter things which have
been kept secret from the foundation of the world.*

Matthew 13:33-35

When Jesus said something was "secret from
the foundation of the world," He was speaking
of the Church. This was never explained in the
Old Testament.

Here is Paul speaking of the same thing:

*Which in other ages was not made known unto
the sons of men, as it is now revealed unto his
holy apostles and prophets by the Spirit; That the
Gentiles should be fellow heirs, and of the same
body, and partakers of his promise in Christ by the
gospel: Whereof I was made a minister, according
to the gift of the grace of God given unto me by
the effectual working of his power. Unto me, who
am less than the least of all saints, is this grace
given, that I should preach among the Gentiles the
unsearchable riches of Christ; And to make all men
see what is the fellowship of the mystery, which
from the beginning of the world hath been hid in
God, who created all things by Jesus Christ:*

Ephesians 3:5-9

This was Paul's greatest honor; it was his privilege
to reveal what was hidden from the Old Testament
writers. It was not the fact that Gentiles can be saved;

they were saved before John the Baptist. No, what he talks about here is the strange mystery that we call the Church. It was only hinted at in the Old Testament, but it was Paul's privilege to reveal it.

The Church was born at Pentecost, but there were some prerequisites to that "birth." The Atonement had to be made (Matthew 16:21). The Resurrection had to occur (Ephesians 1:20-23), and the Ascension had to take place (Ephesians 4:7-11). The spiritual gifts occurred only after the Ascension, and of course, the giving of the Holy Spirit in Acts 2.

What we're talking about here is Ecclesiology, the study of the Church. All kinds of people ask, "Does the Church go through the Tribulation?" There's a big debate amongst scholars over this issue. That's not a problem of Eschatology; it's a problem of Ecclesiology.

Anyone who thinks the Church goes through the Great Tribulation has two pieces of homework. They have to find out the purpose of the Tribulation (via Eschatology), and they also need to define the Church (via Ecclesiology).

The Mystery Character of the Church

We are not talking about buildings when we use the term *Church*. We're talking about the mystery Church: its mystery character. There are at least six things we need to know about the character of the Church.

1) **The Church is the body of Christ.**
There are many members but one body.
The body of Christ in the Scripture is
treated as one: singular. That's the "body"
concept from Ephesians 3.

2) **The Holy Spirit of God is indwelling
every believer.** Paul saw this as a very
radical change from the past. He knew who
the Holy Spirit was; he learned the Old
Testament well under Gamaliel. What he
couldn't grasp was the commitment of the
Holy Spirit to continuously indwell every
believer in the Church. That's absolutely
unique to the Church. That wasn't true
before the Church began, and it won't be
true after the Church is taken away. That's a
special gift to the Church.

3) **The Church is the bride of Christ.**
In Ephesians 5:31, Paul notes that a man
shall be joined to his wife, "and the two
shall be one flesh." Then he says, "This is
a great mystery: but I speak concerning
Christ and the church." The Church is
joined to Christ in a unique and singular
way.[9] Of course, there is also the marriage
supper and ruling and reigning with Christ.

4) **The Church is waiting for the
Bridegroom**, the Lord Jesus, to come
and take her in the *Harpazo*, or Rapture.
First Corinthians 15:50-58 describes this

event and characterizes it as happening, "in the twinkling of an eye, at the last trump." In prophetic terms, this is the next event for the Church to expect.

G.H. Pember was among the first to recognize that Revelation 12 may also deal with the *Harpazo.* That chapter speaks of the woman giving birth to the *man child*, and the man child being caught up to God. Most of us visualize that as the ascension of Christ, but G.H. Pember considered that this might also include the Rapture because the next thing is the Great Tribulation.

5) **The Church is one "new man"** as described in Ephesians 2:15; "for to make in Himself of twain [Jew and Gentile] one new man, so making peace."

6) **The Church is distinguished from both the Jews and Gentiles.** 1 Corinthians 10:32 is an example of that: "Give none offence, neither to the Jews, nor to the Gentiles, nor to the church of God." That distinction evaporates in Revelation 4 and following.

So as we consider the characteristics of the Church and realize that what was hidden in the Old Testament is now revealed, we begin to understand that the world is getting ready now for the big climax, the big finish.

The Blindness of Israel

And when he was come near, he beheld the city,
and wept over it, saying, "If you had known, even
you, especially in this your day, the things that
make for your peace! But now they are hidden
from your eyes."

Luke 19:41-42

Earlier, we saw that this passage helps define the interval between the sixty-nine weeks and the seventieth week. There is more here that we need to consider.

Jesus declares a corporate blindness on the part of Israel. They can't see Jesus; they can't understand who He is. Will this last forever? No, Paul tells us in Romans:

For I would not, brethren, that ye should be
ignorant of this mystery, lest ye should be wise
in your own conceits; that blindness in part is
happened to Israel, until the fulness of the Gentiles
be come in.

Romans 11:25

There are three major "until" statements that stand in the way of the restoration of Israel.[10] This *fullness of the Gentiles* is one of them.

Don't confuse the fullness of the Gentiles with the *times of the Gentiles*. Luke 21 uses "times of the Gentiles" to portray the period from Nebuchadnezzar to the Antichrist. That is the era of Gentile dominion on the planet earth. It had a beginning; it will have an end.

The fullness of the Gentiles is something else; it refers to the Church. There will only be a certain number of believers in the Church, and God knows that number. When that last person believes, making the Church complete, the Father will say to the Son, "Go get them." When they are brought in, that's the end of the interval, and God will once again continue his program for Israel. So the fullness of the Gentiles is synonymous with the Church period, and then the Great Tribulation follows.

Chapter 6
The 70th Week (verse 27)

Let's take a look now, at the climactic verse of the seventieth week prophecy:

> *And he shall confirm the covenant with many for one week: and in the midst of the week he shall cause the sacrifice and the oblation to cease, and for the overspreading of abominations he shall make it desolate, even until the consummation, and that determined shall be poured upon the desolate.*

Daniel 9:27

Who Is This?

Who is the "he" mentioned in this verse? The previous verse mentions both the Messiah, as well as "the prince that shall come." This is very simple grammar; what's the antecedent? It's "the prince that shall come." Some people try to say this "he" is the Messiah, but that doesn't actually fit the text and creates other problems.

This is not the Messiah. "The prince that shall come" will enforce the covenant with the many; that's his role with Israel for this final "week" in the prophecy. Understand, though, he is the bad guy; he's not a savior.

Some would translate the phrase in Daniel 9:27 as "he signs a treaty," but it doesn't say that. The literal translation is "he enforces a covenant" (*enforce* is equivalent to *confirm*).

It might be that he will be associated with a treaty, or he may simply enforce the Land Covenant in Deuteronomy that gives Israel the right to the land. It could be that simple. No matter what he actually does, his "enforcing" defines the seven year period.

In the middle of that seven year period, this *prince* ignores his promise and causes "the sacrifice and the oblation to cease." This implies, obviously, that there is a temple standing, and the Jews have returned to the Levitical system of sacrifices. Building the Temple may not be the subject of the treaty, but it's at least a by-product of it.[11]

This verse also tells us that, "for the overspreading of abominations he shall make it desolate, even until the consummation, and that determined shall be poured upon the desolate." This leader will evidently repeat the circumstance of a Greek leader in 167 B.C.

That was when Antiochus Epiphanes made Torah reading punishable by death. He slaughtered a sow on the altar. He also erected an idol of Zeus in the Holy of Holies, which is defined as the *abomination of desolation*. That's what triggered the Maccabean Revolt against their Seleucid rulers.

Jesus makes reference to this abomination of desolation in a briefing to His disciples

(Matthew 24:15). He was referring to what Antiochus Epiphanes did two centuries earlier, but He was speaking about what would be done in the future by the prince that shall come. It is still an unfulfilled prophecy. Nothing like that has happened since He predicted it; although a Roman emperor did try.

Until the Time Ordained

In 40 A.D., Emperor Caligula sent an order from Rome that his image be established in the Holy of Holies of the Jewish Temple in Jerusalem. Petronius, the general in charge, knew that if he tried to do that there would be an uprising, just like before. So he refused to follow his orders.

When Caligula found out that he didn't do it, he sent an order for Petronius to be killed. It's interesting that within two weeks of sending that order, Caligula died. It "happened" that the news of Caligula's death arrived in Judaea before the order to have Petronius killed, due to some delays at sea.

Not only did God stop Caligula's plans, preserving Petronius in the process; He even went further. He removed the Temple entirely by allowing it to be destroyed by the Romans.

In order for the abomination of desolation to occur, the Temple has to be standing. But God removed it and won't allow another until the time ordained for all these things to take place. We know the Temple will be rebuilt because Daniel, Paul, John and Jesus all make reference to it standing during the end of times.

Something else here is kind of interesting. After Caligula dies, we can follow the succession of emperors and come to a year that amounted to civil war. General Vespasian, the first general in charge at the siege of Jerusalem, emerged from that conflict as emperor and founder of a new dynasty. When he left Jerusalem, he put his son, Titus Vespasian in charge. It was Titus Vespasian who carried out, in 70 A.D., the massacre of Jerusalem and the destruction of the Temple.

Titus Vespasian had just become a prince, since his father had just become the emperor. This could be seen as a sort of "shadow" of the prince that shall come. There are also some authorities who believe that Titus could have been a descendant of Antiochus Epiphanes, who committed the first Abomination of Desolation.[12]

John 10:22

Sometimes we may run across a detail, one of those little tidbits that most people just skip over, and we may not quite understand it. But if we double back and dig a little deeper, we may find some hidden treasure. Here is one of those places where this would apply:

And it was at Jerusalem the feast of the dedication, and it was winter.

John 10:22

How can the Feast of Dedication be in the winter? The dedication of Solomon's Temple is described in 1 Kings 8, and that was in the autumn, not the winter. The second temple, sometimes called Zerubbabel's Temple, was dedicated in the spring according to Ezra 6. We have to refer to extra-biblical sources to discover a winter dedication of the Temple.

It shocks many Christians to realize that Hanukkah is the dedication being referred to in this passage, and that it's being endorsed by the Gospel of John. This goes back to 167 B.C. when the Temple had been defiled by the Greek king, Antiochus Epiphanes, with the abomination of desolation.

Greek Antiochus coin gave way to Jewish Hasmonean coin.

It took three years for the Jews to throw off the Greek Seleucid Empire. Then they had to destroy all the implements that were desecrated, cleanse the Temple, and re-dedicate it to God's service so they could begin the proper sacrifices again. This is celebrated today as Hanukkah—but don't confuse the historical aspect of it with the colorful legend that surrounds it.

Why did the Holy Spirit call our attention to this? Hanukkah seems insignificant. It celebrates an event that's outside any Biblical reference; it occurred between the Old and New Testaments.

The Spirit is saying that we need to understand the events surrounding Antiochus Epiphanes. Referring to that particular Temple dedication offers a hint that it's important. It turns out to be directly related to what Jesus will idiomatically refer to as happening in the future: the abomination of desolation.

Time, Times, and Half a Time

There is a division of the seventieth week that's described in a variety of ways. One that might sound foreign to our ears is found in Daniel 12:7 and Revelation 12:14. It is the phrase: "time, times, and half a time." Revelation is quoting from Daniel, so we have to look at the Aramaic to understand what this means.

It's a way of counting. If we read, "a time and half a time" we would call that one and a half. But we have this other word that reads as "times" in English. It's hard for us to understand because English doesn't have a *dual* number for nouns. We have the singular form and we can make a plural by adding an *s*. There is one exception, though. If someone said "I've invited all of my friends over—both of them," we would probably laugh because we understand that *both* means two. In that sense, *both* is a dual word.

"Times" is a dual word and operates the same way. So if "times" can be counted as two, we add that to the one and a half, and have three and a half as a total. Since a week consists of seven days, we understand this to mean half of the seventieth week, the final week.

In the chart below, there are several ways listed to describe this time: three and a half years; 42 months; 1260 days; half a week. Those are all equivalent phrases and act as a confirmation for the length of time being dealt with in the prophecy.

"Time, Time, and $\frac{1}{2}$ Time"	
• "Times" = dual, later lost in Aramaic	
$1 + 2 + \frac{1}{2} = 3\frac{1}{2}$	Dan 7:25, 12:7; Rev 12:14
• 3 $\frac{1}{2}$ years	Dan 9:27, 12:7
• 42 months	Rev 11:2, 13:5
• 1260 days	Rev 11:3; Dan 12:6
• $\frac{1}{2}$ "weeks"	Dan 9:27

Unquestionably, this is the most documented period of time in the entire Bible. These references are from both the Old and New Testaments. The Holy Spirit has thoroughly documented this peculiar seven year period, the last half of which is the Great Tribulation.

The Great Tribulation

The 70th week is defined by a seven year covenant being enforced by the world leader. In the middle of that "week," in the middle of that seven year period, he erects an image to be worshipped in the Holy of Holies. Jesus spoke about that:

*When ye therefore shall see the abomination
of desolation, spoken of by Daniel the prophet,
stand in the holy place, (whoso readeth, let him
understand:) Then let them which be in Judaea
flee into the mountains:*

Matthew 24:15-16

This will be the beginning of the Great Tribulation, and there are two points to remember about this period. The Great Tribulation is not seven years long; it's the last half of that seven year period. Also, this is prophecy concerning the Jews, not the Church. It's important that we have the right perspective.

Jesus tells those in Judea to flee. Then He describes what's coming:

*For then shall be great tribulation, such as was not
since the beginning of the world to this time, no,
nor ever shall be. And except those days should be
shortened, there should no flesh be saved: but for
the elect's sake those days shall be shortened.*

Matthew 24:21-22

Jesus is quoting, in effect, from the book of Daniel:

*And at that time shall Michael stand up, the
great prince which standeth for the children of thy
people: and there shall be a time of trouble, such
as never was since there was a nation even to that
same time: and at that time thy people shall be
delivered, every one that shall be found written in
the book.*

Daniel 12:1

Jesus is clear when He says the "time of trouble" is unprecedented. That's a terrifying thing to embrace because certainly the Jews have suffered terrible, terrible abuse. One Jew in three on the Earth was killed during the Nazi Holocaust, but the "time of trouble" will be much worse. Zachariah tells us:

> *And it shall come to pass, that in all the land, saith the LORD, two parts therein shall be cut off and die; but the third shall be left therein. And I will bring the third part through the fire, and will refine them as silver is refined, and will try them as gold is tried: they shall call on my name, and I will hear them: I will say, It is my people: and they shall say, The LORD is my God.*

Zechariah 13:8-9

That's horrible. We speak of it as the Great Tribulation because Jesus labels it that way. The "time of Jacob's trouble" is the idiom that Jeremiah uses in his book.

> *Alas! for that day is great, so that none is like it: it is even the time of Jacob's trouble; but he shall be saved out of it.*

Jeremiah 30:7

When Jeremiah speaks of this period as "the time of Jacob's trouble," it helps us to realize this is a worldwide tribulation, but its primary focus is the Jew. There's a very key verse in Hosea:

> *I will go and return to my place, till they*
> *acknowledge their offence, and seek my face:*
> *in their affliction they will seek me early.*
>
> Hosea 5:15

God is speaking here, and says, "I will go and return to my place." How can He return if He hasn't left it? Jesus left, and He will return.

When will He return? He explained it clearly—when "they acknowledge their offense." This is a prerequisite condition to the second coming of Christ. Israel, as a nation, must petition Him to come back. They must acknowledge Jesus as Messiah, and He will then return.

The Prince That Shall Come

We have already commented on "the prince that shall come" in connection with the abomination of desolation. But we need to come back to him in order to better understand how he fits into end-time prophecies.

His Titles

"The prince that shall come" is one of many titles given to this coming world leader. In Genesis 3:15, when God declares war on Satan, this prince is referred to as the "seed of the Serpent." He speaks of the "seed of the woman," a title of Christ, and the "seed of the serpent" for this other-christ.

The "idol shepherd," is another title given to him in Zechariah 11:16, 17. In Daniel 7 and 8, he is called the "little horn." Of course, we have "the prince that shall come" in Daniel 9:26; as well as the "willful king" in Daniel 11. These are all allusions of various kinds from the Old Testament.

There are a total of thirty-three titles for him in the Old Testament, and in the New Testament there are thirteen. He's called the "beast" in Revelation 11 and 13. In 2 Thessalonians 2, Paul calls him the "man of sin" and the "son of perdition" in verse 2; then in verse 8, he says he is the "lawless one."

Jesus alludes to him in John 5:43 as "the one who comes in his own name."

It's interesting, John calls him the antichrist (or pseudo-christ) in 1 John 2, but in all of Revelation, which John also wrote, he doesn't use that title at all; he prefers different terms.

His Characteristics

This leader is an intellectual genius:

And of the ten horns that were in his head, and of the other which came up, and before whom three fell; even of that horn that had eyes, and a mouth that spake very great things, whose look was more stout than his fellows.

Daniel 7:20

And in the latter time of their kingdom, when the transgressors are come to the full, a king of fierce countenance, and understanding dark sentences, shall stand up.

Daniel 8:23

Behold, thou art wiser than Daniel; there is no secret that they can hide from thee:

Ezekiel 28:3

He's a persuasive orator:

And of the ten horns that were in his head, and of the other which came up, and before whom three fell; even of that horn that had eyes, and a mouth that spake very great things, whose look was more stout than his fellows.

Daniel 7:20

And the beast which I saw was like unto a leopard, and his feet were as the feet of a bear, and his mouth as the mouth of a lion: and the dragon gave him his power, and his seat, and great authority.

Revelation 13:2

He's a very shrewd politician:

And in his estate shall stand up a vile person, to whom they shall not give the honour of the kingdom: but he shall come in peaceably, and obtain the kingdom by flatteries.

Daniel 11:21

And through his policy also he shall cause craft to prosper in his hand; and he shall magnify himself

in his heart, and by peace shall destroy many:
he shall also stand up against the Prince of princes;
but he shall be broken without hand.

Daniel 8:25

He's a financial genius:

And it was given unto him to make war with the
saints, and to overcome them: and power was given
him over all kindreds, and tongues, and nations.

Revelation 13:7

With thy wisdom and with thine understanding
thou hast gotten thee riches, and hast gotten gold
and silver into thy treasures: By thy great wisdom
and by thy traffick hast thou increased thy riches,
and thine heart is lifted up because of thy riches:

Ezekiel 28:4-5

Lo, this is the man that made not God his strength;
but trusted in the abundance of his riches,
and strengthened himself in his wickedness.

Psalm 52:7

But in his estate shall he honour the God of forces:
and a god whom his fathers knew not shall he
honour with gold, and silver, and with precious
stones, and pleasant things.

Daniel 11:38

But he shall have power over the treasures of gold
and of silver, and over all the precious things of
Egypt: and the Libyans and the Ethiopians shall
be at his steps.

Daniel 11:43

He's a forceful military leader:

> *And his power shall be mighty, but not by his own*
> *power: and he shall destroy wonderfully, and shall*
> *prosper, and practise, and shall destroy the mighty*
> *and the holy people.*

Daniel 8:24

> *And I saw, and behold a white horse: and he*
> *that sat on him had a bow; and a crown was*
> *given unto him: and he went forth conquering,*
> *and to conquer.*

Revelation 6:2

> *And they worshipped the dragon which gave power*
> *unto the beast: and they worshipped the beast,*
> *saying, Who is like unto the beast? who is able*
> *to make war with him?*

Revelation 13:4

He becomes militarily very powerful but he rises to power on politics and peacemaking. He ends up becoming a very forceful military leader: a very powerful organizer[13] and he's also a unifying religious guru.[14] There are many more descriptions; this could be a whole study.[15] These are just some highlights.

Is He Jew or Gentile?

Is he Jew or Gentile? That's a big question. This leader will be the "son" of Satan;[16] that's clear.

Some believe the leader will be a Jew, based on a number of passages.[17] For instance, John 5:43 reads, "another will come in his own name," and the Greek word used is *allos* not *heteros*. This implies that he's a Jew, not a Gentile. He obviously is received by Israel as Messiah, which implies that he's Jewish.[18] Some believe he will be a Gentile because he's a Roman prince, and there are a number of reasons offered. Just be aware that this is not a settled issue.

The First Beast

Revelation 13 has two players: a political leader and a religious leader. They operate as a duet. Scholars often call this arrangement a *satanic trinity*. Satan's object is to be worshipped as God. So he has his prototype of a son, and he has his prototype of the Holy Spirit. It's a trinity; at least, that's the conception of some scholars.

The first beast, of two, is described in Revelation 13:

> *Then I stood on the sand of the sea. And I saw a beast rising up out of the sea, having seven heads and ten horns, and on his horns ten crowns, and on his heads a blasphemous name. Now the beast which I saw was like a leopard, his feet were like the feet of a bear, and his mouth like the mouth of a lion. The dragon gave him his power, his throne, and great authority.*
>
> Revelation 13:1-2

Does that sound familiar from Daniel? But there is one difference; they are in reverse order. They're backwards because we're looking backward in time, not forward. Revelation 12:9 refers to this dragon as "the red dragon," and identifies him as none other than Satan himself.

Satan can give this leader authority because this is Satan's world. Remember, when Christ was tempted, Satan showed him all the nations of the world, and said:

> *All this power will I give thee, and the glory*
> *of them: for that is delivered unto me; and to*
> *whomsoever I will I give it. If thou therefore wilt*
> *worship me, all shall be thine.*

> Luke 4:6-7

Jesus didn't challenge his ownership, even though Satan is a usurper. In Revelation 5, we see Jesus taking back the title deed to earth, because He purchased it on the cross. That's the most important escrow closing in the universe

His Physical Description

In Revelation 13 we are told:

> *And I saw one of his heads as it were wounded to*
> *death; and his deadly wound was healed: and all*
> *the world wondered after the beast.*

> Revelation 13:3

Did he really die, or did everybody just think he died? Doesn't matter because, whatever it was, it was healed somehow, and "all the world wondered after the beast."

There's only one physical description of this person in the Bible that I know of, and that's in Zechariah 11:17.

> *Woe to the idol shepherd that leaveth the flock!*
> *the sword shall be upon his arm, and upon his*
> *right eye: his arm shall be clean dried up, and his*
> *right eye shall be utterly darkened.*

Zechariah 11:17

That's all we know about his appearance. Some people speculate that the incapacity of the arm and eye recorded here is the result of the head wound referenced in Revelation. In any event, they thought he was dead but he comes back to life somehow, and he has an impairment.

There is conjecture that, as people seek to identify themselves with him, they take his sign on their forehead or on their hand. This would be similar to someone incorporating a characteristic (hairstyle, brand-name clothing, car, *et cetera*) of one of their heroes into their own life in order to identify closely with them.

The Second Beast: The False Prophet

We're still dealing with a duet, so notice the rise of the second beast in Revelation:

> *And I beheld another beast coming up out of the*
> *earth; and he had two horns like a lamb, and he*
> *spake as a dragon. And he exerciseth all the power*
> *of the first beast before him, and causeth the earth*
> *and them which dwell therein to worship the first*
> *beast, whose deadly wound was healed.*

Revelation 13:11-12

We need to be sensitive in the book of Revelation to the precision with which terms are used. "Earth dwellers" aren't just people physically on earth. They're the people who dwell on the earth; they are the losers in this scenario. We can also see the reference to his wound, again, and that it was healed. There is a certainty being given here.

Going to verse 14, we read:

> *And deceiveth them that dwell on the earth by the means of those miracles which he had power to do in the sight of the beast; saying to them that dwell on the earth, that they should make an image to the beast, which had the wound by a sword, and did live.*

Revelation 13:14

Notice this head wound is alluded to three times in the passage. Continuing with the next verses:

> *And he had power to give life unto the image of the beast, that the image of the beast should both speak, and cause that as many as would not worship the image of the beast should be killed. And he causeth all, both small and great, rich and poor, free and bond, to receive a mark in their right hand, or in their foreheads: And that no man might buy or sell, save he that had the mark, or the name of the beast, or the number of his name. Here is wisdom. Let him that hath understanding count the number of the beast: for it is the number of a man; and his number is Six hundred threescore and six.*

Revelation 13:15-18

666

People, who know nothing else about the Bible, know about the 6-6-6 in Revelation. It comes from the passage above, specifically Revelation 13:18.

There have been all kinds of conjectures about this. For instance, the word *Christós* in the Greek has been used in connection with this number. They take the two letters that start and end that word, then put a *xi* (which looks something like a serpent) between them to represent the other letters. In the Greek numbering system (*gematria*) these letters become 600 plus 60 plus 6, or the 666. Of course, that is the type of the antichrist (or pseudo-christ to be more precise.)

There are books spending all their time on barcodes because barcodes use six as a separator symbol, at least in some of them. Then, there are the chips that can be inserted under the skin. Since they can transpond information, there is speculation that they would be used as "the mark." Clearly, these technologies could permit a dictator incredible power, but that's not the point.

Too many people overlook that it is his number, not ours, that's at issue here. It's not a PIN number or a Social Security Number; those numbers are not his. It's his number that people will take visibly as a sign of allegiance to him. They may need to do that in order to get an identity, but it's his number and name that form the critical identity. Credit cards, or whatever other things, are not the issue.

It is clear, though, that anyone taking his identity on their forehead or arm has an absolute barrier to ever being saved. Scripture makes that a certainty.

Israel: God's Timepiece

We know in God's timing it's getting close to the end. There's a fascinating way for this to be illustrated. (We are indebted to Clarence Larkin for first observing this.)

    1) There are four periods involved:

    2) Abraham to the Exodus

    3) Exodus to the Temple

    4) Temple to the Edict of Artaxerxes

    5) Artaxerxes to the Second Coming

Take the years when Israel is out of favor during each period, subtract them from the calendar years for that period, and the answer will be exactly 490 years. ("Out of favor" can refer to being in servitude or exile; these are interruptions of their freedom to serve God.)

The first period was Abraham to the Exodus, and it covered 505 calendar years. We subtract 15 years to count the years when Ishmael was the heir. The total is 490 years.

Next is the Exodus to the dedication of the first Temple. That has 601 calendar years with 111 years subtracted for the time they were in servitude to surrounding nations. This was during the period of the Judges, and there were six of those events. The total is 490 years.

The third period is from the dedication of the Temple to the Edict of Artaxerxes, and that was 560 calendar years. (This is the edict that is the starting point for Daniel's 70 weeks.) Subtract 70 years for the Babylonian captivity and we have 490 years, again.

Finally, we take Artaxerxes' Edict to the Second Coming of Messiah. Obviously, we don't have all of our numbers for this. We do know the numbers for the first 69 weeks of Daniel's 70, though. From the Edict to the birth of Messiah was 483 years. We also know that the final "week" will last seven years. Once again we have 490 years; even though we don't know how long the church interval will last.

So, beginning with Abraham, we have four equal periods of time. Why is that important? If all the calculations are right, this would be a confirmation that world history is coming to a climax. It also confirms that Israel is not only God's timepiece, but they are still an important part of His plans, as well.

The Tribulation and The Rapture

The seventieth week is defined by the antichrist enforcing a covenant. In the middle of that period, he erects the abomination of desolation, which is the trigger for the Jews to flee Jerusalem. From there to the end is the Great Tribulation, which culminates with the battle of Armageddon where Jesus intercedes.

That is His second coming, and then He sets up His millennial reign.

So when does the Rapture take place? There are those who believe the Rapture of the Church takes place at the end; that the Church does go through the Great Tribulation. People who hold that view usually do not know anything about Daniel 9. Their view doesn't fit Daniel's scenario.

There are some who realize that the Church does NOT go through the Great Tribulation. They also recognize that the Great Tribulation starts in the middle of the week. They say that the Church will be taken after the seventieth week begins, but before the Tribulation. People who hold that view are called *mid-trib* people.

There is a variation of that position called *pre-wrath*. It comes from a popular book published by Marvin Rosenthal,[19] but it's basically a variation of the mid-trib position.

Of course, in this book we take the position that the Rapture will take place not only before the Tribulation, but prior to the seventieth week of Daniel. That doesn't mean we're right, but we hold that view.

In fact, please notice that the Rapture doesn't occur at the beginning of the seventieth week. There is an interlude between the Rapture and the beginning of the seventieth week, but we don't know how long it lasts. We do know that the antichrist can't show up until the Rapture takes place.[20] After the antichrist is revealed, some time is needed for him to rise to power so he can enforce this covenant. It might take one day for this to develop, or it might take thirty years; we don't know.

Now, there are also the *post-trib* people. Most of the denominational churches would count themselves as post-trib. There are some inherent problems with that position. First of all, they deny the New Testament teaching of Imminency. All through the New Testament, we're taught to expect Jesus to return for us at any moment. That's called Imminency.

The post-trib view also requires the Church to be on the earth during the seventieth week. But, Daniel's prophecy concerns the Jews, not the church; they are mutually exclusive, so that can't happen. Don't take my word for it; a diligent study will show that Israel and the Church are dealt with separately.

According to post-trib teachers, the Church will experience God's wrath in the Great Tribulation. But, we were promised not to experience His wrath.

> *For God hath not appointed us to wrath, but to obtain salvation by our Lord Jesus Christ,*
>
> 1 Thessalonians 5:9

> *Because thou hast kept the word of my patience, I also will keep thee from the hour of temptation, which shall come upon all the world, to try them that dwell upon the earth.*
>
> Revelation 3:10

How can the bride come with Him if He's coming to gather them? Those events are contradictions. He comes first to gather us back.

There are more problems with this view. Who will populate the millennium if everybody at the Second Coming is either given resurrection bodies or cast into Hades? There is death during the Millennium. There are problems with the people. Who are the "sheep" and "goats" in the Matthew 25 judgment? How can the virgins of Matthew 25 buy oil without the mark of the beast? These aren't big deals but they're problems. This could be a whole study in itself.

The order of events we're discussing is dealt with in 2 Thessalonians. This letter is Paul's response to a forgery that was received in Thessalonica and had really upset the people. They thought they had either been badly taught or they had missed the Rapture. Paul was trying to straighten them out by reminding them what he had taught them about concerning the *day of the Lord.*

> *Let no man deceive you by any means: for that day shall not come, except there come a falling away first, and that man of sin be revealed, the son of perdition; Who opposeth and exalteth himself above all that is called God, or that is worshipped; so that he as God sitteth in the temple of God, shewing himself that he is God.*
>
> 2 Thessalonians 2:3-4

Most people view the "falling away" referred to here as the apostasy, and that's fine. It actually may be a reference to the rapture, but we don't have to insist on that in order to make the case being presented.

> *He who now [restraineth] will [restrain] until He be taken out of the way. And then shall that Wicked [one] be revealed, whom the Lord shall consume with the spirit of his mouth, and shall destroy with the brightness of his coming.*
>
> 2 Thessalonians 2:7-8

So this tells us that the Restrainer must be removed before the "wicked one" can be revealed. We have a whole two-hour Rapture study, with diagrams, on this for those who want to go further into it.[21]

Eschatology and Hermeneutics

Most mainstream Protestant churches, as well as Roman Catholic churches, hold a view called *amillennial*. They don't really focus on the idea of Jesus coming back to rule the planet Earth, from a literal throne in Israel, for a thousand years (a millennium). Yet that's what the Bible literally says in Revelation 20:1-7.

Those who are *pre-millennial* believe there is a millennium. They believe that Jesus is going to literally rule the earth for one thousand years.

There were some who were *post-millennial*. They said that we were already in the millennium. Those views have pretty much died out since World

Wars I and II. Most people recognize we are not in the millennium because there is so much trouble. It's been said, "If we're in the millennium then Satan's chain is too long."

There are three groups who take the millennial view of Christ seriously: the pre-tribs, the mid-tribs, and the post-tribs. It turns out that most churches are amillennial and post-tribulational. Many denominations, and the Roman Catholic Church, would be in that category. People who are regarded as Biblical Fundamentalists are typically pre-millennial and pre-tribulation.

There are good people in each of these camps, so, don't misuse this information; it's not that simple. It turns out, that a person's view of the last days will be derived from their views of hermeneutics, their method of interpretation. The more literally someone takes the Bible, the more seriously they treat the text.

People who have a willingness to be allegorical, to treat these things as just poetry or to be soft in their hermeneutics will swing toward an amillennial, post-tribulational view. So this means a person's hermeneutical perspective can determine their viewpoint. If they're very strict, they take the Bible very seriously and very literally, they will drift toward the millennial, pre-tribulational camp as a point of view.

History of Pre-Tribulational View

The pre-trib view is not a recent idea. There are people claiming that it is, but that's not true. This view is found in the *Epistle of Barnabas* in the first century, Irenaus in *Against Heresies*, Hyppolitus in the second century, and Justin Martyr in *Dialogue with Trypho*.

Perhaps the most interesting, is Ephraem the Syrian in the fourth century. He was a very, very prominent writer in the Byzantine Church. Just a relatively few years ago, some of his work was found and translated. In one of the sermons, he says, "For all the saints and Elect of God are gathered, prior to the tribulation there is to come, and are taken to the Lord lest they see the confusion that is to overwhelm the world because of our sins."[22] That's just a sample allusion. Clearly, he was teaching a pre-trib, pre-millennial viewpoint.

The pre-tribulation eschatology teaching shows up all through the centuries:

Peter Jurieu, The Approaching Deliverance of the Church, 1687

Philip Doddridge, Commentary on the New Testament, 1738

Dr. John Gill, Commentary on the New Testament, 1748

James MacKnight, Commentary on the Apostolical Epistles, 1763

Thomas Scott, Commentary on the Holy Bible, 1792

Emanuel Lacunza (Ben Ezra), 1812

Edward Irving, 1816

John N. Darby, 1820

Margaret McDonald, 1830

It was popularized by L. Edward Irving and John Darby, as well as Margaret McDonald in the early 1800's and some people allege that they invented it. That's not true. They popularized it but it's been around since the first century.

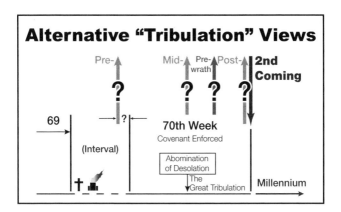

Revelation Architecture

Now, the Revelation architecture would be important to understand here. In Revelation, we have the lamp stands that are identified in chapter one as the Church; they also show up in chapters two and three. In chapter four, the lampstands are in heaven when John arrives; so the Church is in heaven in chapter four.

The twenty-four elders are identified as the redeemed by their songs. They worship the Lamb before He receives the scroll, and it's when He opens the scroll that all these judgments begin. So when these judgments proceed, where are the twenty-four elders? They are in heaven, and that means the Church is in heaven.

The tribulation begins when the scroll is unsealed and, of course, the seventieth week is then detailed from chapter six through chapter nineteen in the book of Revelation. From here, we encourage serious students of the Bible to take on a full study of the book of Revelation.[23]

The point should be made that chapters two and three are the most important chapters. We have the seven churches here: the churches of Ephesus, Smyrna, Pergamos, Thyatira, Sardis, Philadelphia and Laodicea.

There are at least four levels of understanding to each message sent to the individual churches.

1) They were local churches, and they had real problems that are addressed in their message.

2) Each of the seven messages can be taken to heart by every church—in any age.

3) They're also carrying messages that are homiletic; they apply to each of us individually.

4) There is a fourth level: the historical.
   If the churches were in any other order,
   the following descriptions would not
   be true.

Ephesus seems to characterize
   the apostolic church;

Smyrna, the persecuted church;

Pergamos, the married church
   (married to the world);

Thyatira the medieval church;

Sardis, the denominational church;

Philadelphia, the missionary church;

Laodicea, the apostate church.

The first three letters have some peculiar structural characteristics. The promises that are given to them are post-scripted, coming after the conclusion of the letter in a very strange way. In the last four letters, the promises are made in the body of the letter, not as a postscript. Furthermore, the last four letters all had explicit references to the second coming of Christ; the first three do not. Thyatira is given the promise that they will enter the tribulation. Philadelphia is expressly told it will not; it will be gathered out before the time of the tribulation. As for the rest, they are somewhat speculative as to where they fit in the picture but that's something for further study.

Chapter 7
The Doctrine of Imminency

The doctrine of Imminency is another important issue. The dictionary definition of *imminent* is, "ready to take place." Here it refers to the Church's expectation of the next event. Don't confuse that with *immanent*, which means "to be within, or near." God is always with us, even though He is also far above us, or transcendent. Nor should it be confused with *eminent*, which is a title of honor, an outstanding distinction.

The doctrine of Imminency teaches believers to expect the Savior to come from heaven at any moment. Here are examples of Scripture teaching this doctrine:

For our conversation is in heaven; from whence also we look for the Saviour, the Lord Jesus Christ:
Philippians 3:20

Looking for that blessed hope, and the glorious appearing of the great God and our Saviour Jesus Christ;

Titus 2:13

So Christ was once offered to bear the sins of many; and unto them that look for him shall he appear the second time without sin unto salvation.

Hebrews 9:28

And to wait for his Son from heaven, whom he raised from the dead, even Jesus, which delivered us from the wrath to come.

1 Thessalonians 1:10

Wherefore comfort one another with these words.

1 Thessalonians 4:18

Therefore let us not sleep, as do others, but let us watch and be sober.

1 Thessalonians 5:6

He which testifieth these things saith, Surely I come quickly. Amen. Even so, come, Lord Jesus.

Revelation 22:20

Those who hold a mid-trib (pre-wrath) or post-trib viewpoint have to deny the doctrine of Imminency because they require intervening events to occur before His coming.

Imminence conveys hope and a warm expectancy, as 1 Thessalonians 1:10 emphasizes. This teaching pervades the whole New Testament. The doctrine of imminence is intended to result in a victorious and purified life:

Beloved, now are we the sons of God, and it doth not yet appear what we shall be: but we know that, when he shall appear, we shall be like him; for we shall see him as he is. And every man that hath this hope in him purifieth himself, even as he is pure.

1 John 3:2-3

Paul seems to include himself among those who look for Christ's return:

> *For this we say unto you by the word of the Lord, that we which are alive and remain unto the coming of the Lord shall not prevent them which are asleep.*
>
> 1 Thessalonians 4:15

> *Now we beseech you, brethren, by the coming of our Lord Jesus Christ, and by our gathering together unto him,*
>
> 2 Thessalonians 2:1

Near the end of his first letter, Paul admonished Timothy and ended by urging him to continue "until the appearing of our Lord Jesus Christ" (1 Timothy 6:14). Jewish converts were reminded that, "yet a little while, and He that shall come will come, and will not tarry," in Hebrews 10:37.

Two Extremes

There are two extremes in the way people approach Imminence. One is what I call *rapturitis*. These are people who are sure the Rapture is a week from Tuesday, so they don't plan for the future or provide for their families. This happened in the first churches, too. People stopped working and had to be exhorted to return to their jobs, and to have patience:

*For even when we were with you, this we
commanded you, that if any would not work,
neither should he eat. For we hear that there are
some which walk among you disorderly, working
not at all, but are busybodies. Now them that are
such we command and exhort by our Lord Jesus
Christ, that with quietness they work, and eat their
own bread.*

2 Thessalonians 3:10-12

*Be ye also patient; stablish your hearts: for the
coming of the Lord draweth nigh.*

James 5:8

It's right to be expectant, but some people today
are doing the same thing: disengaging from life.
Some won't get behind issues in the community or
country because they're thinking, "We're going to
get raptured out of here next Tuesday, so why should
we bother?" That's the wrong attitude. Jesus gave
us the right attitude in Luke 19:13 when He said,
"Occupy until I come."

Rapturitis is probably a uniquely American
dementia. Since we can prove that the Church will
not go through the Great Tribulation, some of us
arrogantly assume that we will escape what most of the
body of Christ, in most of the world, for most of the
past two thousand years has had to endure. It's called
persecution. Don't confuse tribulation in the general
sense with that specific period of three and a half years,
which is labeled the Great Tribulation. Just because
we know we won't go through the Great Tribulation,

doesn't mean that there might not be really dark days ahead for us here in America.

There are many experts who really believe the body of Christ in America is going to have to go underground. Increasingly, it is politically incorrect to be a Biblical Christian in this country. J. Vernon McGee caught my attention when he predicted that not only will the body of Christ have to go underground, but the attack against them will be led by the denominational churches. That's a shocker. He said that about twenty years ago.

The other extreme is *rapture mania*; these are the date-setters. Hardly a week goes by I don't get a paper from someone who's got some new calculation based on the "signs in the stars," or the most popular shirt sizes, or some other "discovery." They may have a job, but they also have a misguided fixation.

Chapter 8
In Such An Hour

Let's remember what Jesus said:

Therefore be ye also ready: for in such an hour as ye think not the Son of man cometh.

Matthew 24:44

That doesn't mean it's going to take longer than we think. It's going to be sooner than we probably think. I believe you and I are being plunged into that period of time about which the Bible says more than it does about any other time in history; including the time Jesus was among us, walking the shores of Galilee and climbing the mountains of Judea.

However, there are some circumstances that are going to take a little time. The "props" are being moved onto the "set" in preparation for the final act, but it's not quite ready yet. There are certain allies not in position; there are certain things that we expect to see.

To the extent that it looks like we've got some time, we should rejoice because we've got an important opportunity.

Do you know someone you love who has yet to discover the redemption that God has given us through

Christ? I want you to remember that every believer has found the redemption of Christ as a result of someone's prayer.

That's the opportunity of this time that's left to us. You have an opportunity to pray that God will bring these people you love into the kingdom. With every day that goes by, He can bring into their path those influences, those insights, that can cause them to discover the extremes that He has gone to that they might live. God can blindfold their prejudices, their excuses, and bring them into a fellowship with Him that will last throughout eternity.

You want to take that very, very seriously. We still have a little time; Daniel's seventieth week has not begun—yet.

Endnotes

1 There are three important primary prayers in the historical books of the Old Testament: Ezra 9, Nehemiah 9, and Daniel 9. There happens to be a 9 in all three references. That's not of any significance; I think it's just a way to help remember it.

2 Nguyen, Marie-Lan. *Passing Lion*. Brick panel from the Procession Way which ran from the Marduk temple to the Ishtar Gate and the Akitu Temple. Glazed terracotta, reign of Nebuchadrezzar II (605 BC–562 BC) in Babylon (Iraq). USB *Wikipedia Commons*. Paris: Musee du Louvre, 2006.

3 I believe we can apply 2 Chronicles 7:14 to America's predicament, although it's a different one altogether. It reads, "If my people, which are called by My name, shall humble themselves, and pray, and seek my face, and turn from their wicked ways; then will I hear from heaven, and will forgive their sin, and will heal their land."

4 It was a rare, out-of-print book when I was a teenager. A friend of mine happened to have a copy and treated me, as a gift, with Sir Robert Anderson's *The Coming Prince*. I had already accepted Christ. I was a Christian in my teens, but it was this insight that galvanized me to realize you can prove that Jesus Christ is who He said He is by this very passage. It's astonishing.

5 Anderson, Robert. *The Coming Prince*. Grand Rapids, MI.: Kregel, 1984.

6 Asa Hall, with the new telescope of the U.S. Naval Observatory, made history by discovering the two moons of Mars—151 years after Jonathan Swift published his book.

7 See Missler, Chuck. *Prophecy 20/20: Profiling the Future through the Lens of Scripture*. Nashville, Tenn.: Thomas Nelson, 2006.

8   These citations will help you get started on your search
     for references to the interval between weeks 69 and 70
     in Daniel's prophecy: Dan 9:26; Isa 61:1,2 (re: Lk 4:18-
     20); Rev 12:5,6. Also: Isa 54:7; Hos 3:4,5; Amos 9:10,11
     (Acts 15:13-18); Micah 5:2,3; Zech 9:9,10; Lk 1:31,32;
     21:24.

9   John 17:23 describes this union as he prays for us to the
     Father: "I in them, and Thou in Me, that they may be made
     perfect in one…" Two verses earlier, Jesus prays, "that they
     also may be one in Us…"

10   Three "Untils" of Israel for Restoration: Romans 11:25
     "Until the fullness of the Gentiles be brought in";
     Hosea 5:15 "Until they acknowledge their offence…";
     Luke 21:24 "Until the times of the Gentiles are fulfilled."

11   Jews today have a great dilemma; they have no remedy
     for sin. Leviticus 17:11 and Hebrews 9:22 say that,
     "without the shedding of blood, there is no remission of
     sin." Where can they shed blood when they have no Temple?
     They have a tremendous consciousness of their sin, yet
     they don't have a remedy. This dilemma caused the Jews,
     at the Council of Jamnia, to redefine Judaism. They turned
     it into what we would call Talmudic Judaism, which is
     a far cry from the Judaism of Moses (Mosaic Judaism).
     That was their answer to having no temple and not being
     able to practice the Law.

12   While many of the royal families intermarried, making it
     possible for Titus to be a descendent, I don't know if that's
     true. It wouldn't surprise me, though, if the antichrist who
     does show up will have some surprising credentials because
     he's going to pass himself off in pretty sterling terms to the
     whole world.

13   Revelation 13:1,2; 17:17

14   2 Thessalonians 2:4; Revelation 13:3,14,15

15   Psalm 10, 52, 55; Isaiah 10,11,13,14; Jeremiah 49-51; Zechariah 5; Revelation 18

16   Genesis 3:14; Isaiah 27:1; Ezekiel 28:12-19; Revelation 13.

17   Ezekiel 21:25-27; Ezekiel 28:2-10 (of the circumcision); Daniel 11:36,37; John 5:43

18   Psalm 55

19   Rosenthal, Marvin J. *The Pre-Wrath Rapture of the Church.* Nashville: Thomas Nelson, 1990.

20   See 2 Thessalonians 2:6-8.

21   Missler, Chuck. *The Rapture: Christianity's Most Preposterous Belief.* Post Falls, ID: Koinonia House, 2010.

22   The English translation of the Latin text in C.P. Caspari's *Briefe, Abhandlungen und Predigten aus den zwei letzten Jahrhunderten des kirchlichen Altertums und dem Anfang des Mittelater* (Christiania, 1890, pp. 208-20) was provided by Cameron Rhoades, instructor of Latin at Tyndale Theological Seminary, Ft. Worth, TX. See also: Missler, Chuck. "Byzantine Text Discovery: Ephraem The Syrian." Koinonia House. http://www.khouse.org/articles/1995/39/#notes.

23   See Chuck Missler's study materials on Revelation at https://resources.khouse.org/revelation/

Bibliography

Anderson, Robert. *The Coming Prince*. Grand Rapids, MI.:
    Kregel, 1984.

Baldwin, Joyce G. *Daniel: Tyndale Old Testament
    Commentaries*. Downers Grove, IL: Inter-Varsity Press,
    1978.

Barnes, Albert. *Notes on the Old Testament Explanatory and
    Practical: Daniel Vol. 2*. Edited by Robert Frew. Vol. 2.
    Grand Rapids, MI: Baker Book House, 1950.

Bloomfield, Arthur E. *The End of the Days*. Minneapolis, MN:
    Bethany Fellowship, 1961.

Culver, Robert D. *Daniel and the Latter Days*. Chicago, IL:
    Moody Press, 1954.

DeHaan, Martin R. *Daniel the Prophet*. Grand Rapids, MI:
    Zondervan Publishing House, 1947.

Driver, Samuel R. *The Book of Daniel*. Cambridge: University
    Press, 1900.

Faucsset, A.R. *The Book of Daniel, A Critical and Experimental
    Commentary, Vol. IV*. Grand Rapids, MI: Wm. B.
    Eerdmans, 1945.

Gaebelein, Arno C. *The Prophet Daniel*. New York: Our Hope
    Publishers, 1911.

Hartman, Louis F., and Alexander A. DiLella. *The Book of
    Daniel*. Garden City, New York: Doubleday & Company,
    1977.

Ironside, Henry A. *Lectures on Daniel the Prophet*. New York:
    Loizeaux Bros., 1920.

Keil, Carl F. *The Book of the Prophet Daniel, Biblical
    Commentary on the Old Testament*. Translated by M.G.
    Easton. Edinburgh, Scotland: T. & T. Clark, 1891.

Larkin, Clarence. *The Book of Daniel*. Philadelphia PA: Clarence Larkin, 1929.

Leupold, Herbert C. *Exposition of Daniel*, Grand Rapids MI: Baker Book House, 1969.

McClain, Alva J. *Daniel's Prophecy of the Seventy Weeks*. Grand Rapids, MI: Zondervan Publishing House, 1940.

Newell, Philip R. *Daniel: the Man Greatly Beloved and His Prophecies*. Chicago, IL: Moody Press, 1962.

Nguyen,Marie-Lan. *Passing lion, brick panel from the Procession Way which ran from the Marduk temple to the Ishtar Gate and the Akitu Temple*. Glazed terracotta, reign of Nebuchadnezzar II (605 BC–562 BC), Babylon (Iraq). *Wikipedia Commons*, photo. Paris: Musee du Louvre, 2006

Pusey, Edward B. *Daniel the Prophet.*, New York: Funk & Wagnalls, 1891.

Strauss, Lehman. *The Prophecies of Daniel*. Neptune, NJ: Loizeaux Bros., 1965.

Walvoord, John F. *Daniel, The Key to Prophetic Revelation*. Chicago, IL : Moody Press, 1971.

Whitcomb, John C., Jr. *Darius the Mede*. Grand Rapids, MI: Wm. B. Eerdmans, 1959.

Wilson, Robert Dick. *Studies in the Book of Daniel*. Grand Rapids, MI: Baker Book House, 1979.

Wiseman, Donad J. *The Chronicles of the Chaldean Kings (626-556B.C.)*. London: Trustees of the British Museum, 1956.

Wood, Leon. *A Commentary on Daniel*. Grand Rapids, MI: Zondervan, 1973

Midrach Yalkut Shimoni: Torah, Nevi'im, u-Khetuvim. Jerusalem: Machon HaMeor, 2001.

Young, Edward J. *The Prophecy of Daniel*. Grand Rapids, MI: Wm. B. Eerdmans, 1949.